Personal D

Name:

Address:

Phone Number:

Email:

In case of an emergency

Emergency Contact 1:

Phone Number:

Emergency Contact 2:

Phone Number:

Medical Conditions:

Allergies:

Blood Type:

Date of Birth:

Additional Information

Welcome

Thank you for buying this book. As a small independent creator it's really appreciated! I always love to hear feedback so I can keep improving my diaries and make them as useful to you as possible. If you could leave a review on Amazon it would not only help me develop newer versions of this book but it also help a small fry publisher like me standout from the crowd.

Wishing you the best of adventures!

Feedback Notes

Contents

1:
2:
3:
4:
5:
6:
7:
8:
9:
10:
11:
12:
13:
14:
15:
16:
17:
18:
19:
20:
21:
22:
23:
24:
25:
26:
27:
28:
29:
30:
31:
32:
33:
34:
35:
36:
37:
38:
39:
40:
41:
42:
43:
44:
45:
46:
47:
48:
49:
50:

Date:

M T W T F S S

Name:

Area:

Busy / Quiet

____ °C

Journey

Journey Time: | Car Parking:
Transport Type: | Free: ☐ Charge: ☐ £: _____

Toilets: ☐ Cafe: ☐

Hike

Start: | Distance: | Elevation:
Finish: | Duration: | Difficulty:

Hike Type: Loop   Out & Back   One Way   Day Hike   Multi-Day:

Navigation (Map/App):

Phone Signal:

Terrain:

Wild Camp: ☐ 📍
Wild Swim: ☐ 📍

Food (pub/foraging):

Water:

Wild Life:

Notes:

Companions, highlights, hardships......:

Technical Kit:

Kit Issues:

Wish had taken:

Sketch, photo...

Date: M T W T F S S

Name:

Area:

Busy / Quiet

___ °C

Journey
Journey Time: Car Parking:
Transport Type: Free: ☐   Charge: ☐   £: _____

Toilets: ☐   Cafe: ☐

Hike
Start: Distance: Elevation:
Finish: Duration: Difficulty:

Hike Type: Loop   Out & Back   One Way   Day Hike   Multi-Day:

Navigation (Map/App):

Phone Signal:

Terrain:

Wild Camp: ☐ 📍
Wild Swim: ☐ 📍

Food (pub/foraging):

Water:

Wild Life:

Notes:

Companions, highlights, hardships......:

Technical Kit:

Kit Issues:

Wish had taken:

Sketch, photo...

Date:

M T W T F S S

Name:

Area:

Busy / Quiet

___ °C

Journey

Journey Time: Car Parking:

Transport Type: Free: ☐ Charge: ☐ £:_____

Toilets: ☐   Cafe: ☐

Hike

Start: Distance: Elevation:

Finish: Duration: Difficulty:

Hike Type: Loop   Out & Back   One Way   Day Hike   Multi-Day:

Navigation (Map/App):

Phone Signal:

Terrain:

Wild Camp: ☐ 📍
Wild Swim: ☐ 📍

Food (pub/foraging):

Water:

Wild Life:

Notes:

Companions, highlights, hardships......:

Technical Kit:

Kit Issues:

Wish had taken:

Sketch, photo...

Date:

M T W T F S S

Name:

Area:

Busy / Quiet

 ___ °C

Journey Time:	Car Parking:	Journey
Transport Type:	Free: ☐ Charge: ☐ £:	

Toilets: ☐   Cafe: ☐

Hike	Start:	Distance:	Elevation:
	Finish:	Duration:	Difficulty:

Hike Type: Loop   Out & Back   One Way   Day Hike   Multi-Day:

Navigation (Map/App):

Phone Signal:

Terrain:

Wild Camp: ☐ 📍
Wild Swim: ☐ 📍

Food (pub/foraging):

Water:

Wild Life:

Notes:

Companions, highlights, hardships……:

Technical Kit:

Kit Issues:

Wish had taken:

Sketch, photo…

Date:

Name:

Area:

M T W T F S S

Busy / Quiet

___ °C

Journey Time:	Car Parking:	Journey
Transport Type:	Free: ☐ Charge: ☐ £:	

Toilets: ☐   Cafe: ☐

Hike	Start:	Distance:	Elevation:
	Finish:	Duration:	Difficulty:

Hike Type: Loop   Out & Back   One Way   Day Hike   Multi-Day:

Navigation (Map/App):

Phone Signal:

Terrain:

Wild Camp: ☐ 📍
Wild Swim: ☐ 📍

Food (pub/foraging):

Water:

Wild Life:

Notes:

Companions, highlights, hardships......:

Technical Kit:

Kit Issues:

Wish had taken:

Sketch, photo...

Date:

M T W T F S S

Name:

Area:

Busy / Quiet

 ___°C

Journey
- Journey Time:
- Car Parking:
- Transport Type:
- Free: ☐   Charge: ☐   £:_____

Toilets: ☐   Cafe: ☐

Hike
- Start:
- Distance:
- Elevation:
- Finish:
- Duration:
- Difficulty:

Hike Type: Loop   Out & Back   One Way   Day Hike   Multi-Day:

Navigation (Map/App):

Phone Signal:

Terrain:

Wild Camp: ☐ 📍
Wild Swim: ☐ 📍

Food (pub/foraging):

Water:

Wild Life:

Notes:

Companions, highlights, hardships......:

Technical Kit:

Kit Issues:

Wish had taken:

Sketch, photo...

Date:

M T W T F S S

Name:

Area:

Busy / Quiet

___ °C

Journey

Journey Time: Car Parking:

Transport Type: Free: ☐ Charge: ☐ £: ....

Toilets: ☐ Cafe: ☐

Hike

Start: Distance: Elevation:

Finish: Duration: Difficulty:

Hike Type: Loop Out & Back One Way Day Hike Multi-Day:

Navigation (Map/App):

Phone Signal:

Terrain:

Wild Camp: ☐ 📍
Wild Swim: ☐ 📍

Food (pub/foraging):

Water:

Wild Life:

Notes:

Companions, highlights, hardships......:

Technical Kit:

Kit Issues:

Wish had taken:

Sketch, photo...

Date:

M T W T F S S

Name:

Area:

Busy / Quiet

___ °C

Journey

Journey Time: Car Parking:
Transport Type: Free: ☐   Charge: ☐   £:

Toilets: ☐   Cafe: ☐

Hike

Start: Distance: Elevation:
Finish: Duration: Difficulty:

Hike Type: Loop   Out & Back   One Way   Day Hike   Multi-Day:

Navigation (Map/App):

Phone Signal:

Terrain:

Wild Camp: ☐
Wild Swim: ☐

Food (pub/foraging):

Water:

Wild Life:

Notes:

Companions, highlights, hardships......:

Technical Kit:

Kit Issues:

Wish had taken:

Sketch, photo...

Date:
M T W T F S S

Name:
Area:
Busy / Quiet

 ___ °C

Journey

Journey Time: Car Parking:
Transport Type: Free: ☐   Charge: ☐   £: _____

Toilets: ☐   Cafe: ☐

Hike

Start: Distance: Elevation:
Finish: Duration: Difficulty:

Hike Type: Loop   Out & Back   One Way   Day Hike   Multi-Day:

Navigation (Map/App):

Phone Signal:

Terrain:

Wild Camp: ☐ 📍
Wild Swim: ☐ 📍

Food (pub/foraging):

Water:

Wild Life:

Notes:

Companions, highlights, hardships......:

Technical Kit:

Kit Issues:

Wish had taken:

Sketch, photo...

Date:

Name:

Area:

M T W T F S S

Busy / Quiet

___ °C

Journey Time:	Car Parking:	
Transport Type:	Free: ☐ Charge: ☐ £: _____	Journey

Toilets: ☐ Cafe: ☐

Hike	Start:	Distance:	Elevation:
	Finish:	Duration:	Difficulty:

Hike Type: Loop   Out & Back   One Way   Day Hike   Multi-Day:

Navigation (Map/App):

Phone Signal:

Terrain:

Wild Camp: ☐ 📍
Wild Swim: ☐ 📍

Food (pub/foraging):

Water:

Wild Life:

Notes:

Companions, highlights, hardships......:

Technical Kit:

Kit Issues:

Wish had taken:

Sketch, photo...

Date:

M T W T F S S

Name:

Area:

Busy / Quiet

____ °C

Journey

Journey Time: Car Parking:

Transport Type: Free: ☐   Charge: ☐   £: _____

Toilets: ☐   Cafe: ☐

Hike

Start: Distance: Elevation:

Finish: Duration: Difficulty:

Hike Type: Loop   Out & Back   One Way   Day Hike   Multi-Day:

Navigation (Map/App):

Phone Signal:

Terrain:

Wild Camp: ☐ 📍
Wild Swim: ☐ 📍

Food (pub/foraging):

Water:

Wild Life:

Notes:

Companions, highlights, hardships……:

Technical Kit:

Kit Issues:

Wish had taken:

Sketch, photo...

Date: | Name:
M T W T F S S

Area:

Busy / Quiet

___ °C

Journey Time:	Car Parking:	
Transport Type:	Free: ☐ Charge: ☐ £:	Journey

Toilets: ☐ Cafe: ☐

Hike	Start:	Distance:	Elevation:
	Finish:	Duration:	Difficulty:

Hike Type: Loop   Out & Back   One Way   Day Hike   Multi-Day:

Navigation (Map/App):

Phone Signal:

Terrain:

Wild Camp: ☐ 📍
Wild Swim: ☐ 📍

Food (pub/foraging):

Water:

Wild Life:

Notes:

Companions, highlights, hardships……:

Technical Kit:

Kit Issues:

Wish had taken:

Sketch, photo…

Date:

M T W T F S S

Name:

Area:

Busy / Quiet

_____ °C

Journey

Journey Time:	Car Parking:
Transport Type:	Free: ☐ Charge: ☐ £: _____

Toilets: ☐   Cafe: ☐

Hike

Start:	Distance:	Elevation:
Finish:	Duration:	Difficulty:

Hike Type: Loop   Out & Back   One Way   Day Hike   Multi-Day:

Navigation (Map/App):

Phone Signal:

Terrain:

Wild Camp: ☐ 📍
Wild Swim: ☐ 📍

Food (pub/foraging):

Water:

Wild Life:

Notes:

Companions, highlights, hardships......:

Technical Kit:

Kit Issues:

Wish had taken:

Sketch, photo...

Date:
M T W T F S S

Name:
Area:
⬅───────────────────────➡
Busy / Quiet

🌡 ___ °C ☀ ⛅ ☁ 🌧 ⛈ ❄

Journey
| Journey Time: | Car Parking: |
| Transport Type: | Free: ☐ Charge: ☐ £: _____ |

Toilets: ☐   Cafe: ☐

Hike
| Start: | Distance: | Elevation: |
| Finish: | Duration: | Difficulty: |

Hike Type: Loop   Out & Back   One Way   Day Hike   Multi-Day:

Navigation (Map/App):

Phone Signal:

Terrain:

Wild Camp: ☐ 📍
Wild Swim: ☐ 📍

Food (pub/foraging):

Water:

Wild Life:

Notes:

Companions, highlights, hardships......:

Technical Kit:

Kit Issues:

Wish had taken:

Sketch, photo...

Date:
M T W T F S S

Name:

Area:

Busy / Quiet

 ___ °C

Journey

Journey Time:	Car Parking:
Transport Type:	Free: ☐ Charge: ☐ £: _____

Toilets: ☐   Cafe: ☐

Hike

Start:	Distance:	Elevation:
Finish:	Duration:	Difficulty:

Hike Type: Loop   Out & Back   One Way   Day Hike   Multi-Day:

Navigation (Map/App):

Phone Signal:

Terrain:

Wild Camp: ☐ 📍
Wild Swim: ☐ 📍

Food (pub/foraging):

Water:

Wild Life:

Notes:

Companions, highlights, hardships......:

Technical Kit:

Kit Issues:

Wish had taken:

Sketch, photo...

Date:

M T W T F S S

Name:

Area:

Busy / Quiet

___ °C

Journey

Journey Time: Car Parking:
Transport Type: Free: ☐ Charge: ☐ £: ....

Toilets: ☐ Cafe: ☐

Hike

Start: Distance: Elevation:
Finish: Duration: Difficulty:

Hike Type: Loop Out & Back One Way Day Hike Multi-Day:

Navigation (Map/App):

Phone Signal:

Terrain:

Wild Camp: ☐ 📍
Wild Swim: ☐ 📍

Food (pub/foraging):

Water:

Wild Life:

Notes:

Companions, highlights, hardships......:

Technical Kit:

Kit Issues:

Wish had taken:

Sketch, photo...

Date:

M T W T F S S

Name:

Area:

Busy / Quiet

_____ °C

Journey Time:	Car Parking:	Journey
Transport Type:	Free: ☐ Charge: ☐ £: _____	

Toilets: ☐   Cafe: ☐

Hike
Start:	Distance:	Elevation:
Finish:	Duration:	Difficulty:

Hike Type: Loop   Out & Back   One Way   Day Hike   Multi-Day:

Navigation (Map/App):

Phone Signal:

Terrain:

Wild Camp: ☐ 📍
Wild Swim: ☐ 📍

Food (pub/foraging):

Water:

Wild Life:

Notes:

Companions, highlights, hardships......:

Technical Kit:

Kit Issues:

Wish had taken:

Sketch, photo...

Date: M T W T F S S

Name:

Area:

Busy / Quiet

____ °C

| Journey Time: | Car Parking: | Journey |
| Transport Type: | Free: ☐ Charge: ☐ £: | |

Toilets: ☐   Cafe: ☐

| Hike | Start: | Distance: | Elevation: |
| | Finish: | Duration: | Difficulty: |

Hike Type: Loop   Out & Back   One Way   Day Hike   Multi-Day:

Navigation (Map/App):

Phone Signal:

Terrain:

Wild Camp: ☐ 📍
Wild Swim: ☐ 📍

Food (pub/foraging):

Water:

Wild Life:

Notes:

Companions, highlights, hardships......:

Technical Kit:

Kit Issues:

Wish had taken:

Sketch, photo...

Date:

M T W T F S S

Name:

Area:

Busy / Quiet

___ °C

Journey Time:	Car Parking:	
Transport Type:	Free: ☐ Charge: ☐ £:............	Journey

Toilets: ☐ Cafe: ☐

	Start:	Distance:	Elevation:
Hike	Finish:	Duration:	Difficulty:

Hike Type: Loop   Out & Back   One Way   Day Hike   Multi-Day:

Navigation (Map/App):

Phone Signal:

Terrain:

Wild Camp: ☐ 📍
Wild Swim: ☐ 📍

Food (pub/foraging):

Water:

Wild Life:

Notes:

Companions, highlights, hardships......:

Technical Kit:

Kit Issues:

Wish had taken:

Sketch, photo...

Date:

Name: ←――――――――――――――――――――→

Area:

M T W T F S S

Busy / Quiet

____ °C

Journey

Journey Time:	Car Parking:
Transport Type:	Free: ☐ Charge: ☐ £: _____

Toilets: ☐   Cafe: ☐

Hike

Start:	Distance:	Elevation:
Finish:	Duration:	Difficulty:

Hike Type: Loop   Out & Back   One Way   Day Hike   Multi-Day:

Navigation (Map/App):

Phone Signal:

Terrain:

Wild Camp: ☐ 📍
Wild Swim: ☐ 📍

Food (pub/foraging):

Water:

Wild Life:

Notes:

Companions, highlights, hardships......:

Technical Kit:

Kit Issues:

Wish had taken:

Sketch, photo...

Date: M T W T F S S

Name:

Area:

Busy / Quiet

____ °C

Journey

Journey Time: | Car Parking:
Transport Type: | Free: ☐ Charge: ☐ £: ....

Toilets: ☐   Cafe: ☐

Hike

Start: | Distance: | Elevation:
Finish: | Duration: | Difficulty:

Hike Type: Loop   Out & Back   One Way   Day Hike   Multi-Day:

Navigation (Map/App):

Phone Signal:

Terrain:

Wild Camp: ☐ ⚲
Wild Swim: ☐ ⚲

Food (pub/foraging):

Water:

Wild Life:

Notes:

Companions, highlights, hardships......:

Technical Kit:

Kit Issues:

Wish had taken:

Sketch, photo...

Date: M T W T F S S

Name:

Area:

Busy / Quiet

____ °C

Journey
Journey Time: Car Parking:
Transport Type: Free: ☐   Charge: ☐   £: ....

Toilets: ☐   Cafe: ☐

Hike
Start: Distance: Elevation:
Finish: Duration: Difficulty:

Hike Type: Loop   Out & Back   One Way   Day Hike   Multi-Day:

Navigation (Map/App):

Phone Signal:

Terrain:

Wild Camp: ☐ 📍
Wild Swim: ☐ 📍

Food (pub/foraging):

Water:

Wild Life:

Notes:

Companions, highlights, hardships......:

Technical Kit:

Kit Issues:

Wish had taken:

Sketch, photo...

Date:

Name:

Area:

M T W T F S S

Busy / Quiet

____ °C

Journey

Journey Time: | Car Parking:
Transport Type: | Free: ☐ Charge: ☐ £: ....

Toilets: ☐   Cafe: ☐

Hike

Start: | Distance: | Elevation:
Finish: | Duration: | Difficulty:

Hike Type: Loop   Out & Back   One Way   Day Hike   Multi-Day:

Navigation (Map/App):

Phone Signal:

Terrain:

Wild Camp: ☐ 📍
Wild Swim: ☐ 📍

Food (pub/foraging):

Water:

Wild Life:

Notes:

Companions, highlights, hardships......:

Technical Kit:

Kit Issues:

Wish had taken:

Sketch, photo...

Date:

Name:

Area:

M T W T F S S

Busy / Quiet

___ °C

Journey

Journey Time: Car Parking:

Transport Type: Free: ☐   Charge: ☐   £: ___

Toilets: ☐   Cafe: ☐

Hike

Start: Distance: Elevation:

Finish: Duration: Difficulty:

Hike Type: Loop   Out & Back   One Way   Day Hike   Multi-Day:

Navigation (Map/App):

Phone Signal:

Terrain:

Wild Camp: ☐ 📍
Wild Swim: ☐ 📍

Food (pub/foraging):

Water:

Wild Life:

Notes:

Companions, highlights, hardships......:

Technical Kit:

Kit Issues:

Wish had taken:

Sketch, photo...

Date:

M T W T F S S

Name:

Area:

Busy / Quiet

____ °C

Journey

Journey Time: Car Parking:

Transport Type: Free: ☐   Charge: ☐   £: ....

Toilets: ☐   Cafe: ☐

Hike

Start: Distance: Elevation:

Finish: Duration: Difficulty:

Hike Type: Loop   Out & Back   One Way   Day Hike   Multi-Day:

Navigation (Map/App):

Phone Signal:

Terrain:

Wild Camp: ☐ 📍
Wild Swim: ☐ 📍

Food (pub/foraging):

Water:

Wild Life:

Notes:

Companions, highlights, hardships……:

Technical Kit:

Kit Issues:

Wish had taken:

Sketch, photo…

Date:
M T W T F S S

Name:

Area:

Busy / Quiet

____ °C

Journey
Journey Time: Car Parking:
Transport Type: Free: ☐   Charge: ☐   £: _____

Toilets: ☐   Cafe: ☐

Hike
Start: Distance: Elevation:
Finish: Duration: Difficulty:

Hike Type: Loop   Out & Back   One Way   Day Hike   Multi-Day:

Navigation (Map/App):
Phone Signal:
Terrain:

Wild Camp: ☐ 📍
Wild Swim: ☐ 📍

Food (pub/foraging):
Water:
Wild Life:

Notes:

Companions, highlights, hardships......:

Technical Kit:

Kit Issues:

Wish had taken:

Sketch, photo...

Date: Name:

M T W T F S S

Area:

Busy / Quiet

____ °C

Journey

Journey Time: Car Parking:

Transport Type: Free: ☐   Charge: ☐   £:_____

Toilets: ☐   Cafe: ☐

Hike

Start: Distance: Elevation:

Finish: Duration: Difficulty:

Hike Type: Loop   Out & Back   One Way   Day Hike   Multi-Day:

Navigation (Map/App):

Phone Signal:

Terrain:

Wild Camp: ☐
Wild Swim: ☐

Food (pub/foraging):

Water:

Wild Life:

Notes:

Companions, highlights, hardships......:

Technical Kit:

Kit Issues:

Wish had taken:

Sketch, photo...

Date:

M T W T F S S

Name:

Area:

Busy / Quiet

_____ °C

Journey

Journey Time: Car Parking:

Transport Type: Free: ☐   Charge: ☐   £: _____

Toilets: ☐   Cafe: ☐

Hike

Start: Distance: Elevation:

Finish: Duration: Difficulty:

Hike Type: Loop   Out & Back   One Way   Day Hike   Multi-Day:

Navigation (Map/App):

Phone Signal:

Terrain:

Wild Camp: ☐ 📍
Wild Swim: ☐ 📍

Food (pub/foraging):

Water:

Wild Life:

Notes:

Companions, highlights, hardships......:

Technical Kit:

Kit Issues:

Wish had taken:

Sketch, photo...

Date:

M T W T F S S

Name:

Area:

Busy / Quiet

_____ °C

Journey Time:	Car Parking:	Journey
Transport Type:	Free: ☐ Charge: ☐ £: _____	

Toilets: ☐   Cafe: ☐

Hike	Start:	Distance:	Elevation:
	Finish:	Duration:	Difficulty:

Hike Type: Loop   Out & Back   One Way   Day Hike   Multi-Day:

Navigation (Map/App):

Phone Signal:

Terrain:

Wild Camp: ☐
Wild Swim: ☐

Food (pub/foraging):

Water:

Wild Life:

Notes:

Companions, highlights, hardships......:

Technical Kit:

Kit Issues:

Wish had taken:

Sketch, photo...

Date: M T W T F S S

Name:

Area:

Busy / Quiet

_____ °C

Journey
- Journey Time:
- Car Parking:
- Transport Type:
- Free: ☐ Charge: ☐ £: _____

Toilets: ☐   Cafe: ☐

Hike
- Start: Distance: Elevation:
- Finish: Duration: Difficulty:

Hike Type: Loop   Out & Back   One Way   Day Hike   Multi-Day:

Navigation (Map/App):

Phone Signal:

Terrain:

Wild Camp: ☐
Wild Swim: ☐

Food (pub/foraging):

Water:

Wild Life:

Notes:

Companions, highlights, hardships......:

Technical Kit:

Kit Issues:

Wish had taken:

Sketch, photo...

Date:

M T W T F S S

Name:

Area:

Busy / Quiet

____ °C

Journey
- Journey Time: _____ Car Parking: _____
- Transport Type: _____ Free: ☐ Charge: ☐ £: _____

Toilets: ☐   Cafe: ☐

Hike
- Start: _____ Distance: _____ Elevation: _____
- Finish: _____ Duration: _____ Difficulty: _____

Hike Type: Loop   Out & Back   One Way   Day Hike   Multi-Day:

Navigation (Map/App):

Phone Signal:

Terrain:

Wild Camp: ☐
Wild Swim: ☐

Food (pub/foraging):

Water:

Wild Life:

Notes:

Companions, highlights, hardships......:

Technical Kit:

Kit Issues:

Wish had taken:

Sketch, photo...

Date:

M T W T F S S

Name:

Area:

Busy / Quiet

____ °C

Journey

Journey Time: Car Parking:
Transport Type: Free: ☐   Charge: ☐   £: _____

Toilets: ☐   Cafe: ☐

Hike

Start: Distance: Elevation:
Finish: Duration: Difficulty:

Hike Type: Loop   Out & Back   One Way   Day Hike   Multi-Day:

Navigation (Map/App):

Phone Signal:

Terrain:

Wild Camp: ☐
Wild Swim: ☐

Food (pub/foraging):

Water:

Wild Life:

Notes:

Companions, highlights, hardships......:

Technical Kit:

Kit Issues:

Wish had taken:

Sketch, photo...

Date:

M T W T F S S

Name:

Area:

Busy / Quiet

____ °C

Journey Time:	Car Parking:				Journey
Transport Type:	Free: ☐	Charge: ☐	£:		

Toilets: ☐ Cafe: ☐

Hike	Start:	Distance:	Elevation:
	Finish:	Duration:	Difficulty:

Hike Type: Loop   Out & Back   One Way   Day Hike   Multi-Day:

Navigation (Map/App):

Phone Signal:

Terrain:

Wild Camp: ☐ 📍
Wild Swim: ☐ 📍

Food (pub/foraging):

Water:

Wild Life:

Notes:

Companions, highlights, hardships……:

Technical Kit:

Kit Issues:

Wish had taken:

Sketch, photo…

Date:

M T W T F S S

Name:

Area:

Busy / Quiet

____ °C

Journey Time:	Car Parking:	
Transport Type:	Free: ☐ Charge: ☐ £: _____	Journey

Toilets: ☐   Cafe: ☐

Hike	Start:	Distance:	Elevation:
	Finish:	Duration:	Difficulty:

Hike Type: Loop   Out & Back   One Way   Day Hike   Multi-Day:

Navigation (Map/App):

Phone Signal:

Terrain:

Wild Camp: ☐ 📍
Wild Swim: ☐ 📍

Food (pub/foraging):

Water:

Wild Life:

Notes:

Companions, highlights, hardships......:

Technical Kit:

Kit Issues:

Wish had taken:

Sketch, photo...

Date: M T W T F S S

Name: ⟵───────────────────⟶

Area:

Busy / Quiet

🌡 ___ °C ☀ ⛅ 🌥 🌧 ⛈ ❄

Journey

Journey Time:	Car Parking:
Transport Type:	Free: ☐ Charge: ☐ £: _____

Toilets: ☐   Cafe: ☐

Hike

Start:	Distance:	Elevation:
Finish:	Duration:	Difficulty:

Hike Type: Loop   Out & Back   One Way   Day Hike   Multi-Day:

Navigation (Map/App):

Phone Signal:

Terrain:

Wild Camp: ☐ 📍
Wild Swim: ☐ 📍

Food (pub/foraging):

Water:

Wild Life:

Notes:

Companions, highlights, hardships......:

Technical Kit:

Kit Issues:

Wish had taken:

Sketch, photo...

Date:

M T W T F S S

Name:

Area:

Busy / Quiet

___ °C

Journey

Journey Time: Car Parking:

Transport Type: Free: ☐   Charge: ☐   £: _____

Toilets: ☐   Cafe: ☐

Hike

Start: Distance: Elevation:

Finish: Duration: Difficulty:

Hike Type: Loop   Out & Back   One Way   Day Hike   Multi-Day:

Navigation (Map/App):

Phone Signal:

Terrain:

Wild Camp: ☐ 📍
Wild Swim: ☐ 📍

Food (pub/foraging):

Water:

Wild Life:

Notes:

Companions, highlights, hardships......:

Technical Kit:

Kit Issues:

Wish had taken:

Sketch, photo...

Date:

Name:

Area:

M T W T F S S

Busy / Quiet

____ °C

Journey
Journey Time: Car Parking:
Transport Type: Free: ☐   Charge: ☐   £:............

Toilets: ☐   Cafe: ☐

Hike
Start: Distance: Elevation:
Finish: Duration: Difficulty:

Hike Type: Loop   Out & Back   One Way   Day Hike   Multi-Day:

Navigation (Map/App):

Phone Signal:

Terrain:

Wild Camp: ☐
Wild Swim: ☐

Food (pub/foraging):

Water:

Wild Life:

Notes:

Companions, highlights, hardships......:

Technical Kit:

Kit Issues:

Wish had taken:

Sketch, photo...

Date:

M T W T F S S

Name:

Area:

Busy / Quiet

____ °C

Journey
Journey Time: Car Parking:
Transport Type: Free: ☐ Charge: ☐ £:_____

Toilets: ☐   Cafe: ☐

Hike
Start: Distance: Elevation:
Finish: Duration: Difficulty:

Hike Type: Loop Out & Back One Way Day Hike Multi-Day:

Navigation (Map/App):

Phone Signal:

Terrain:

Wild Camp: ☐ 📍
Wild Swim: ☐ 📍

Food (pub/foraging):

Water:

Wild Life:

Notes:

Companions, highlights, hardships......:

Technical Kit:

Kit Issues:

Wish had taken:

Sketch, photo...

Date:

M T W T F S S

Name:

Area:

Busy / Quiet

_____ °C

Journey

Journey Time: Car Parking:

Transport Type: Free: ☐   Charge: ☐   £: _____

Toilets: ☐   Cafe: ☐

Hike

Start: Distance: Elevation:

Finish: Duration: Difficulty:

Hike Type: Loop   Out & Back   One Way   Day Hike   Multi-Day:

Navigation (Map/App):

Phone Signal:

Terrain:

Wild Camp: ☐ 📍
Wild Swim: ☐ 📍

Food (pub/foraging):

Water:

Wild Life:

Notes:

Companions, highlights, hardships......:

Technical Kit:

Kit Issues:

Wish had taken:

Sketch, photo...

Date:

M T W T F S S

Name:

Area:

Busy / Quiet

____ °C

Journey

Journey Time: Car Parking:

Transport Type: Free: ☐   Charge: ☐   £: ....

Toilets: ☐   Cafe: ☐

Hike

Start: Distance: Elevation:

Finish: Duration: Difficulty:

Hike Type: Loop   Out & Back   One Way   Day Hike   Multi-Day:

Navigation (Map/App):

Phone Signal:

Terrain:

Wild Camp: ☐ 📍
Wild Swim: ☐ 📍

Food (pub/foraging):

Water:

Wild Life:

Notes:

Companions, highlights, hardships......:

Technical Kit:

Kit Issues:

Wish had taken:

Sketch, photo...

Date:

Name:

Area:

M T W T F S S

Busy / Quiet

___ °C

Journey	Journey Time:	Car Parking:
	Transport Type:	Free: ☐ Charge: ☐ £: ....

Toilets: ☐   Cafe: ☐

Hike	Start:	Distance:	Elevation:
	Finish:	Duration:	Difficulty:

Hike Type: Loop   Out & Back   One Way   Day Hike   Multi-Day:

Navigation (Map/App):

Phone Signal:

Terrain:

Wild Camp: ☐ 📍
Wild Swim: ☐ 📍

Food (pub/foraging):

Water:

Wild Life:

Notes:

Companions, highlights, hardships......:

Technical Kit:

Kit Issues:

Wish had taken:

Sketch, photo...

Date: M T W T F S S

Name:

Area:

Busy / Quiet

____ °C

Journey
Journey Time: Car Parking:
Transport Type: Free: ☐ Charge: ☐ £: ....

Toilets: ☐   Cafe: ☐

Hike
Start: Distance: Elevation:
Finish: Duration: Difficulty:

Hike Type: Loop   Out & Back   One Way   Day Hike   Multi-Day:

Navigation (Map/App):
Phone Signal:
Terrain:

Wild Camp: ☐ 📍
Wild Swim: ☐ 📍

Food (pub/foraging):
Water:
Wild Life:

Notes:

Companions, highlights, hardships......:

Technical Kit:

Kit Issues:

Wish had taken:

Sketch, photo...

Date:

Name:

Area:

M T W T F S S

Busy / Quiet

___ °C

Journey

Journey Time: Car Parking:

Transport Type: Free: ☐   Charge: ☐   £: ....

Toilets: ☐   Cafe: ☐

Hike

Start: Distance: Elevation:

Finish: Duration: Difficulty:

Hike Type: Loop   Out & Back   One Way   Day Hike   Multi-Day:

Navigation (Map/App):

Phone Signal:

Terrain:

Wild Camp: ☐ 📍
Wild Swim: ☐ 📍

Food (pub/foraging):

Water:

Wild Life:

Notes:

Companions, highlights, hardships......:

Technical Kit:

Kit Issues:

Wish had taken:

Sketch, photo...

Date:
M T W T F S S

Name:
Area:
Busy / Quiet

___ °C

Journey Time:	Car Parking:			
Transport Type:	Free: ☐	Charge: ☐	£:	

Journey

Toilets: ☐   Cafe: ☐

Hike
Start:	Distance:	Elevation:
Finish:	Duration:	Difficulty:

Hike Type: Loop   Out & Back   One Way   Day Hike   Multi-Day:

Navigation (Map/App):
Phone Signal:
Terrain:

Wild Camp: ☐ 📍
Wild Swim: ☐ 📍

Food (pub/foraging):
Water:
Wild Life:

Notes:

Companions, highlights, hardships......:

Technical Kit:

Kit Issues:

Wish had taken:

Sketch, photo...

Date:

M T W T F S S

Name:

Area:

Busy / Quiet

___ °C

Journey
Journey Time: | Car Parking:
Transport Type: | Free: ☐ Charge: ☐ £: ....

Toilets: ☐   Cafe: ☐

Hike
Start: | Distance: | Elevation:
Finish: | Duration: | Difficulty:

Hike Type: Loop   Out & Back   One Way   Day Hike   Multi-Day:

Navigation (Map/App):

Phone Signal:

Terrain:

Wild Camp: ☐ 📍
Wild Swim: ☐ 📍

Food (pub/foraging):

Water:

Wild Life:

Notes:

Companions, highlights, hardships......:

Technical Kit:

Kit Issues:

Wish had taken:

Sketch, photo...

Date:

M T W T F S S

Name:

Area:

Busy / Quiet

____ °C

Journey

Journey Time: | Car Parking:
Transport Type: | Free: ☐ Charge: ☐ £: _____

Toilets: ☐   Cafe: ☐

Hike

Start: | Distance: | Elevation:
Finish: | Duration: | Difficulty:

Hike Type: Loop   Out & Back   One Way   Day Hike   Multi-Day:

Navigation (Map/App):

Phone Signal:

Terrain:

Wild Camp: ☐ 📍
Wild Swim: ☐ 📍

Food (pub/foraging):

Water:

Wild Life:

Notes:

Companions, highlights, hardships......:

Technical Kit:

Kit Issues:

Wish had taken:

Sketch, photo...

Date:

M T W T F S S

Name:

Area:

Busy / Quiet

____ °C

Journey

Journey Time:	Car Parking:
Transport Type:	Free: ☐ Charge: ☐ £:

Toilets: ☐   Cafe: ☐

Hike

Start:	Distance:	Elevation:
Finish:	Duration:	Difficulty:

Hike Type: Loop   Out & Back   One Way   Day Hike   Multi-Day:

Navigation (Map/App):

Phone Signal:

Terrain:

Wild Camp: ☐ 📍
Wild Swim: ☐ 📍

Food (pub/foraging):

Water:

Wild Life:

Notes:

Companions, highlights, hardships……:

Technical Kit:

Kit Issues:

Wish had taken:

Sketch, photo…

Date:

M T W T F S S

Name:

Area:

Busy / Quiet

___ °C

Journey

Journey Time: Car Parking:

Transport Type: Free: ☐   Charge: ☐   £:

Toilets: ☐   Cafe: ☐

Hike

Start: Distance: Elevation:

Finish: Duration: Difficulty:

Hike Type: Loop   Out & Back   One Way   Day Hike   Multi-Day:

Navigation (Map/App):

Phone Signal:

Terrain:

Wild Camp: ☐ 📍
Wild Swim: ☐ 📍

Food (pub/foraging):

Water:

Wild Life:

Notes:

Companions, highlights, hardships......:

Technical Kit:

Kit Issues:

Wish had taken:

Sketch, photo...

Date:

M T W T F S S

Name:

Area:

Busy / Quiet

____ °C

Journey

Journey Time: Car Parking:

Transport Type: Free: ☐   Charge: ☐   £: ....

Toilets: ☐   Cafe: ☐

Hike

Start: Distance: Elevation:

Finish: Duration: Difficulty:

Hike Type: Loop   Out & Back   One Way   Day Hike   Multi-Day:

Navigation (Map/App):

Phone Signal:

Terrain:

Wild Camp: ☐ 📍

Wild Swim: ☐ 📍

Food (pub/foraging):

Water:

Wild Life:

Notes:

Companions, highlights, hardships......:

Technical Kit:

Kit Issues:

Wish had taken:

Sketch, photo...

Date:
M T W T F S S

Name:

Area:

Busy / Quiet

___ °C

Journey
- Journey Time:
- Transport Type:
- Car Parking:
- Free: ☐ Charge: ☐ £: _____

Toilets: ☐   Cafe: ☐

Hike
- Start:
- Finish:
- Distance:
- Duration:
- Elevation:
- Difficulty:

Hike Type: Loop   Out & Back   One Way   Day Hike   Multi-Day:

Navigation (Map/App):

Phone Signal:

Terrain:

Wild Camp: ☐ 📍
Wild Swim: ☐ 📍

Food (pub/foraging):

Water:

Wild Life:

Notes:

Companions, highlights, hardships......:

Technical Kit:

Kit Issues:

Wish had taken:

Sketch, photo...